My Witchy Planner

By Violet Hummingbird

D1520232

Contents

Welcome to your Witchy Planner!

This planner is designed to help you plan out your magickal practice and feel inspired each day. Included are optional prompts, such as filling in the moon phase, recording a daily tarot or oracle card draw, and writing any astrological or observed energies to align with "today's energy". Also included are some prompts for connecting to your inner self: write if you remember anything from your dreams, an affirmation or list of words to embody, and something you're grateful for.

In the back of the planner, there is free space to write insights, doodle, make lists, anything you wish - in categories such as esbats, sabbats, and notes from divination and study.

Date: / /

Today's Energy_____

Intention_____

Today's Card_____

Dream

Keywords_____

_____.

Affirmations_____

_____.

Gratitude_____

_____.

Moon Phase:

My Practice:

-
-
-

Date: / /

Today's Energy_____

Intention_____

Today's Card_____

Dream

Keywords_____

_____.

Affirmations_____

_____.

Gratitude_____

_____.

Moon Phase:

My Practice:

-
-
-

Date: / /

Today's Energy_____

Intention_____

Today's Card_____

Dream

Keywords_____

_____.

Affirmations_____

_____.

Gratitude_____

_____.

Moon Phase:

My Practice:

•

•

•

Date: / /

Today's Energy_____

Intention_____

Today's Card_____

Dream

Keywords_____

_____.

Affirmations_____

_____.

Gratitude_____

_____.

Moon Phase:

My Practice:

•

•

•

Date: / /

Today's Energy_____

Intention_____

Today's Card_____

Dream

Keywords_____

_____.

Affirmations_____

_____.

Gratitude_____

_____.

Moon Phase:

My Practice:

-
-
-

Date: / /

Today's Energy_____

Intention_____

Today's Card_____

Dream

Keywords_____

_____.

Affirmations_____

_____.

Gratitude_____

_____.

Moon Phase:

My Practice:

-
-
-

Date: / /
Today's Energy_____
Intention_____
Today's Card_____

Dream
Keywords_____
_____.
Affirmations_____
_____.
Gratitude_____
_____.

Moon Phase:

My Practice:

•
•
•

Date: / /
Today's Energy_____
Intention_____
Today's Card_____

Dream
Keywords_____
_____.
Affirmations_____
_____.
Gratitude_____
_____.

Moon Phase:

My Practice:

•
•
•

8

Date: / /

Today's Energy_____

Intention_____

Today's Card_____

Dream

Keywords_____

_____.

Affirmations_____

_____.

Gratitude_____

_____.

Moon Phase:

My Practice:

·

·

·

Date: / /

Today's Energy_____

Intention_____

Today's Card_____

Dream

Keywords_____

_____.

Affirmations_____

_____.

Gratitude_____

_____.

Moon Phase:

My Practice:

·

·

·

9

Date: / /   Moon Phase:
Today's Energy_____
Intention_____
Today's Card_____

Dream
Keywords_____
_____.   My Practice:
Affirmations_____
                                  •
_____.   •
Gratitude_____   •
_____.

Date: / /   Moon Phase:
Today's Energy_____
Intention_____
Today's Card_____

Dream
Keywords_____
_____.   My Practice:
Affirmations_____
                                  •
_____.   •
Gratitude_____   •
_____.

Date: / /   Moon Phase:
Today's Energy_____
Intention_____
Today's Card_____

Dream
Keywords_____

_____.   My Practice:

Affirmations_____   •

_____.   •

Gratitude_____   •

_____.

Date: / /   Moon Phase:
Today's Energy_____
Intention_____
Today's Card_____

Dream
Keywords_____

_____.   My Practice:

Affirmations_____   •

_____.   •

Gratitude_____   •

_____.

Date: / /   Moon Phase:
Today's Energy_____
Intention_____
Today's Card_____

Dream
Keywords_____
_____.   My Practice:
Affirmations_____   •
_____.   •
Gratitude_____   •
_____.

Date: / /   Moon Phase:
Today's Energy_____
Intention_____
Today's Card_____

Dream
Keywords_____
_____.   My Practice:
Affirmations_____   •
_____.   •
Gratitude_____   •
_____.

Date: / /

Today's Energy_____

Intention_____

Today's Card_____

Dream

Keywords_____

_____.

Affirmations_____

_____.

Gratitude_____

_____.

Moon Phase:

My Practice:

.

.

.

Date: / /

Today's Energy_____

Intention_____

Today's Card_____

Dream

Keywords_____

_____.

Affirmations_____

_____.

Gratitude_____

_____.

Moon Phase:

My Practice:

.

.

.

Date: / /   Moon Phase:
Today's Energy_____
Intention_____
Today's Card_____

Dream
Keywords_____
                                             My Practice:
_____.
Affirmations_____   .
                                             .
_____.   .
Gratitude_____
_____.

Date: / /   Moon Phase:
Today's Energy_____
Intention_____
Today's Card_____

Dream
Keywords_____
                                             My Practice:
_____.
Affirmations_____   .
                                             .
_____.   .
Gratitude_____
_____.

Date: / /   Moon Phase:

Today's Energy_____

Intention_____

Today's Card_____

Dream

Keywords_____

_____.   My Practice:

Affirmations_____   .

_____.   .

Gratitude_____   .

_____.

Date: / /   Moon Phase:

Today's Energy_____

Intention_____

Today's Card_____

Dream

Keywords_____

_____.   My Practice:

Affirmations_____   .

_____.   .

Gratitude_____   .

_____.

Date: / /   Moon Phase:
Today's Energy_____
Intention_____
Today's Card_____

Dream
Keywords_____
_____.   My Practice:
Affirmations_____
                                          •
_____.   •
Gratitude_____   •
_____.

Date: / /   Moon Phase:
Today's Energy_____
Intention_____
Today's Card_____

Dream
Keywords_____
_____.
Affirmations_____   My Practice:
                                          •
_____.   •
Gratitude_____   •
_____.

16

Date: / /

Today's Energy_____

Intention_____

Today's Card_____

Dream

Keywords_____

_____.

Affirmations_____   •

_____.   •

Gratitude_____   •

_____.

Moon Phase:

My Practice:

Date: / /

Today's Energy_____

Intention_____

Today's Card_____

Dream

Keywords_____

_____.

Affirmations_____   •

_____.   •

Gratitude_____   •

_____.

Moon Phase:

My Practice:

Date: /   /
Today's Energy_____
Intention_____
Today's Card_____

Dream
Keywords_____
_____.
Affirmations_____
_____.
Gratitude_____
_____.

Moon Phase:

My Practice:

- •
- •
- •

Date: /   /
Today's Energy_____
Intention_____
Today's Card_____

Dream
Keywords_____
_____.
Affirmations_____
_____.
Gratitude_____
_____.

Moon Phase:

My Practice:

- •
- •
- •

Date: / /   Moon Phase:

Today's Energy_____

Intention_____

Today's Card_____

Dream

Keywords_____

_____.   My Practice:

Affirmations_____   .

_____.   .

Gratitude_____   .

_____.

Date: / /   Moon Phase:

Today's Energy_____

Intention_____

Today's Card_____

Dream

Keywords_____

_____.   My Practice:

Affirmations_____   .

_____.   .

Gratitude_____   .

_____.

19

Date: / /

Today's Energy_____

Intention_____

Today's Card_____

Dream

Keywords_____

_____.

Affirmations_____

_____.

Gratitude_____

_____.

Moon Phase:

My Practice:

•

•

•

Date: / /

Today's Energy_____

Intention_____

Today's Card_____

Dream

Keywords_____

_____.

Affirmations_____

_____.

Gratitude_____

_____.

Moon Phase:

My Practice:

•

•

•

Date: / /

Today's Energy_____

Intention_____

Today's Card_____

Dream

Keywords_____

_____.

Affirmations_____

_____.

Gratitude_____

_____.

Moon Phase:

My Practice:

- .
- .
- .

Date: / /

Today's Energy_____

Intention_____

Today's Card_____

Dream

Keywords_____

_____.

Affirmations_____

_____.

Gratitude_____

_____.

Moon Phase:

My Practice:

- .
- .
- .

Date: / /
Today's Energy_____
Intention_____
Today's Card_____

Dream
Keywords_____
_____.
Affirmations_____
_____.
Gratitude_____
_____.

Moon Phase:

My Practice:

•
•
•

Date: / /
Today's Energy_____
Intention_____
Today's Card_____

Dream
Keywords_____
_____.
Affirmations_____
_____.
Gratitude_____
_____.

Moon Phase:

My Practice:

•
•
•

Date: / /
Today's Energy_____
Intention_____
Today's Card_____

Dream
Keywords_____

_____.
Affirmations_____   •

_____.   •
Gratitude_____   •

_____.

Moon Phase:

My Practice:

Date: / /
Today's Energy_____
Intention_____
Today's Card_____

Dream
Keywords_____

_____.
Affirmations_____   •

_____.   •
Gratitude_____   •

_____.

Moon Phase:

My Practice:

Date: / /   Moon Phase:
Today's Energy_____
Intention_____
Today's Card_____

Dream
Keywords_____
_____.   My Practice:
Affirmations_____   •
_____.   •
Gratitude_____   •
_____.

Date: / /   Moon Phase:
Today's Energy_____
Intention_____
Today's Card_____

Dream
Keywords_____
_____.
Affirmations_____   •
_____.   •
Gratitude_____   •
_____.

My Practice:

24

Date: / /   Moon Phase:
Today's Energy_____
Intention_____
Today's Card_____

Dream
Keywords_____

_____.
Affirmations_____   .   My Practice:
                                              .
_____.   .
Gratitude_____   .

_____.

Date: / /   Moon Phase:
Today's Energy_____
Intention_____
Today's Card_____

Dream
Keywords_____

_____.
Affirmations_____   .
                                              .   My Practice:
_____.   .
Gratitude_____   .

_____.

25

Date: / /

Today's Energy_____

Intention_____

Today's Card_____

Dream

Keywords_____

_____.

Affirmations_____

_____.

Gratitude_____

_____.

Moon Phase:

My Practice:

•

•

•

Date: / /

Today's Energy_____

Intention_____

Today's Card_____

Dream

Keywords_____

_____.

Affirmations_____

_____.

Gratitude_____

_____.

Moon Phase:

My Practice:

•

•

•

Date: / /   Moon Phase:
Today's Energy_____
Intention_____
Today's Card_____

Dream
Keywords_____
_____.
Affirmations_____   .
_____.   .
Gratitude_____   .
_____.

My Practice:

Date: / /   Moon Phase:
Today's Energy_____
Intention_____
Today's Card_____

Dream
Keywords_____
_____.
Affirmations_____   .
_____.   .
Gratitude_____   .
_____.

My Practice:

27

Date: / /   Moon Phase:
Today's Energy_____
Intention_____
Today's Card_____

Dream
Keywords_____
_____.   My Practice:
Affirmations_____   •
_____.   •
Gratitude_____   •
_____.

Date: / /   Moon Phase:
Today's Energy_____
Intention_____
Today's Card_____

Dream
Keywords_____
_____.   My Practice:
Affirmations_____   •
_____.   •
Gratitude_____   •
_____.

28

Date: / /   Moon Phase:
Today's Energy_____
Intention_____
Today's Card_____

Dream
Keywords_____

_____.   My Practice:
Affirmations_____   •
                                •
_____.   •
Gratitude_____

_____.

Date: / /   Moon Phase:
Today's Energy_____
Intention_____
Today's Card_____

Dream
Keywords_____

_____.
Affirmations_____   •
                                •
_____.   •
Gratitude_____

_____.

Date: / /
Today's Energy_____
Intention_____
Today's Card_____

Dream
Keywords_____
_____.
Affirmations_____
_____.
Gratitude_____
_____.

Moon Phase:

My Practice:

-
-
-

Date: / /
Today's Energy_____
Intention_____
Today's Card_____

Dream
Keywords_____
_____.
Affirmations_____
_____.
Gratitude_____
_____.

Moon Phase:

My Practice:

-
-
-

Date: / /

Today's Energy_____

Intention_____

Today's Card_____

Dream

Keywords_____

_____.

Affirmations_____

_____.

Gratitude_____

_____.

Moon Phase:

My Practice:

.
.
.

Date: / /

Today's Energy_____

Intention_____

Today's Card_____

Dream

Keywords_____

_____.

Affirmations_____

_____.

Gratitude_____

_____.

Moon Phase:

My Practice:

.
.
.

Date: / /   Moon Phase:
Today's Energy_____
Intention_____
Today's Card_____

Dream
Keywords_____
_____.   My Practice:
Affirmations_____   •
_____.   •
Gratitude_____   •
_____.

Date: / /   Moon Phase:
Today's Energy_____
Intention_____
Today's Card_____

Dream
Keywords_____
_____.   My Practice:
Affirmations_____   •
_____.   •
Gratitude_____   •
_____.

Date: / /
Today's Energy_____
Intention_____
Today's Card_____

Dream
Keywords_____
_____.
Affirmations_____
_____.
Gratitude_____
_____.

Moon Phase:

My Practice:

•
•
•

Date: / /
Today's Energy_____
Intention_____
Today's Card_____

Dream
Keywords_____
_____.
Affirmations_____
_____.
Gratitude_____
_____.

Moon Phase:

My Practice:

•
•
•

33

Date: / /

Today's Energy_____

Intention_____

Today's Card_____

Dream

Keywords_____

_____.

Affirmations_____

_____.

Gratitude_____

_____.

Moon Phase:

My Practice:

-
-
-

Date: / /

Today's Energy_____

Intention_____

Today's Card_____

Dream

Keywords_____

_____.

Affirmations_____

_____.

Gratitude_____

_____.

Moon Phase:

My Practice:

-
-
-

Date: / /   Moon Phase:

Today's Energy_____

Intention_____

Today's Card_____

Dream

Keywords_____

_____.   My Practice:

Affirmations_____   •

_____.   •

Gratitude_____   •

_____.

Date: / /   Moon Phase:

Today's Energy_____

Intention_____

Today's Card_____

Dream

Keywords_____

_____.   My Practice:

Affirmations_____   •

_____.   •

Gratitude_____   •

_____.

Date: / /   Moon Phase:
Today's Energy_____
Intention_____
Today's Card_____

Dream
Keywords_____
                                     My Practice:
_____.
Affirmations_____   •
_____.   •
Gratitude_____   •
_____.

Date: / /   Moon Phase:
Today's Energy_____
Intention_____
Today's Card_____

Dream
Keywords_____
                                     My Practice:
_____.
Affirmations_____   •
_____.   •
Gratitude_____   •
_____.

Date: / /

Today's Energy_____

Intention_____

Today's Card_____

Dream

Keywords_____

_____.

Affirmations_____

_____.

Gratitude_____

_____.

Moon Phase:

My Practice:

- •
- •
- •

Date: / /

Today's Energy_____

Intention_____

Today's Card_____

Dream

Keywords_____

_____.

Affirmations_____

_____.

Gratitude_____

_____.

Moon Phase:

My Practice:

- •
- •
- •

Date: / /   Moon Phase:
Today's Energy_____
Intention_____
Today's Card_____

Dream
Keywords_____
_____.   My Practice:
Affirmations_____
                                    •
_____.   •
Gratitude_____   •
_____.

Date: / /   Moon Phase:
Today's Energy_____
Intention_____
Today's Card_____

Dream
Keywords_____
_____.   My Practice:
Affirmations_____
                                    •
_____.   •
Gratitude_____   •
_____.

38

Date: / /   Moon Phase:
Today's Energy_____
Intention_____
Today's Card_____

Dream
Keywords_____

_____.   My Practice:

Affirmations_____   .

_____.   .

Gratitude_____   .

_____.

Date: / /   Moon Phase:
Today's Energy_____
Intention_____
Today's Card_____

Dream
Keywords_____

_____.   My Practice:

Affirmations_____   .

_____.   .

Gratitude_____   .

_____.

Date: / /

Today's Energy_____

Intention_____

Today's Card_____

Dream

Keywords_____

_____.

Affirmations_____

_____.

Gratitude_____

_____.

Moon Phase:

My Practice:

.
.
.

Date: / /

Today's Energy_____

Intention_____

Today's Card_____

Dream

Keywords_____

_____.

Affirmations_____

_____.

Gratitude_____

_____.

Moon Phase:

My Practice:

.
.
.

Date: / /

Today's Energy_____

Intention_____

Today's Card_____

Dream

Keywords_____

_____.

Affirmations_____

_____.

Gratitude_____

_____.

Moon Phase:

My Practice:

•

•

•

Date: / /

Today's Energy_____

Intention_____

Today's Card_____

Dream

Keywords_____

_____.

Affirmations_____

_____.

Gratitude_____

_____.

Moon Phase:

My Practice:

•

•

•

Date: / /   Moon Phase:
Today's Energy_____
Intention_____
Today's Card_____

Dream
Keywords_____
                                     My Practice:
_____.
Affirmations_____   .
                                     .
_____.   .
Gratitude_____   .
_____.

Date: / /   Moon Phase:
Today's Energy_____
Intention_____
Today's Card_____

Dream
Keywords_____

_____.   My Practice:
Affirmations_____   .
                                     .
_____.   .
Gratitude_____   .
_____.

Date: / /   Moon Phase:
Today's Energy_____
Intention_____
Today's Card_____

Dream
Keywords_____

_____.   My Practice:

Affirmations_____   •

_____.   •

Gratitude_____   •

_____.

Date: / /   Moon Phase:
Today's Energy_____
Intention_____
Today's Card_____

Dream
Keywords_____

_____.

Affirmations_____   •

_____.   •

Gratitude_____   •

_____.

Date: / /   Moon Phase:
Today's Energy_____
Intention_____
Today's Card_____

Dream
Keywords_____

_____.   My Practice:
Affirmations_____
                                                    •
_____.   •
Gratitude_____   •

_____.

Date: / /   Moon Phase:
Today's Energy_____
Intention_____
Today's Card_____

Dream
Keywords_____

_____.
Affirmations_____   My Practice:

_____.   •
Gratitude_____   •
                                                    •
_____.

44

Date: / /
Today's Energy_____
Intention_____
Today's Card_____

Dream
Keywords_____
_____.
Affirmations_____
_____.
Gratitude_____
_____.

Moon Phase:

My Practice:

.
.
.

Date: / /
Today's Energy_____
Intention_____
Today's Card_____

Dream
Keywords_____
_____.
Affirmations_____
_____.
Gratitude_____
_____.

Moon Phase:

My Practice:

.
.
.

Date: / /   Moon Phase:
Today's Energy_____
Intention_____
Today's Card_____

Dream
Keywords_____
_____.   My Practice:
Affirmations_____   ·
_____.   ·
Gratitude_____   ·
_____.

Date: / /   Moon Phase:
Today's Energy_____
Intention_____
Today's Card_____

Dream
Keywords_____
_____.
Affirmations_____   ·   My Practice:
_____.   ·
Gratitude_____   ·
_____.

Date: / /   Moon Phase:
Today's Energy_____
Intention_____
Today's Card_____

Dream
Keywords_____
_____.   My Practice:
Affirmations_____   .
_____.   .
Gratitude_____   .
_____.

Date: / /   Moon Phase:
Today's Energy_____
Intention_____
Today's Card_____

Dream
Keywords_____
_____.   My Practice:
Affirmations_____   .
_____.   .
Gratitude_____   .
_____.

47

Date: / /
Today's Energy_____
Intention_____
Today's Card_____

Dream
Keywords_____

_____.

Affirmations_____

_____.

Gratitude_____

_____.

Moon Phase:

My Practice:

·
·
·

Date: / /
Today's Energy_____
Intention_____
Today's Card_____

Dream
Keywords_____

_____.

Affirmations_____

_____.

Gratitude_____

_____.

Moon Phase:

My Practice:

·
·
·

48

Date: / /

Today's Energy_____

Intention_____

Today's Card_____

Dream
Keywords_____

_____

Affirmations_____

_____

Gratitude_____

_____

Moon Phase:

My Practice:

·
·
·

Date: / /

Today's Energy_____

Intention_____

Today's Card_____

Dream
Keywords_____

_____

Affirmations_____

_____

Gratitude_____

_____

Moon Phase:

My Practice:

·
·
·

Date: / /   Moon Phase:
Today's Energy_____
Intention_____
Today's Card_____

Dream
Keywords_____
_____.   My Practice:
Affirmations_____
_____.   •
Gratitude_____   •
_____.   •

Date: / /   Moon Phase:
Today's Energy_____
Intention_____
Today's Card_____

Dream
Keywords_____
_____.   My Practice:
Affirmations_____   •
_____.   •
Gratitude_____   •
_____.

Date: / /   Moon Phase:
Today's Energy_____
Intention_____
Today's Card_____

Dream
Keywords_____
_____.   My Practice:
Affirmations_____   •
_____.   •
Gratitude_____   •
_____.

Date: / /   Moon Phase:
Today's Energy_____
Intention_____
Today's Card_____

Dream
Keywords_____
_____.   My Practice:
Affirmations_____   •
_____.   •
Gratitude_____   •
_____.

Date: / /
Today's Energy_____
Intention_____
Today's Card_____

Dream
Keywords_____

_____.
Affirmations_____

_____.
Gratitude_____

_____.

Moon Phase:

My Practice:

·
·
·

Date: / /
Today's Energy_____
Intention_____
Today's Card_____

Dream
Keywords_____

_____.
Affirmations_____

_____.
Gratitude_____

_____.

Moon Phase:

My Practice:

·
·
·

Date: / /   Moon Phase:
Today's Energy_____
Intention_____
Today's Card_____

Dream
Keywords_____

_____.   My Practice:

Affirmations_____   .
                                       .
_____.   .
Gratitude_____   .

_____.

Date: / /   Moon Phase:
Today's Energy_____
Intention_____
Today's Card_____

Dream
Keywords_____

_____.   My Practice:

Affirmations_____   .
                                       .
_____.   .
Gratitude_____   .

_____.

Date: / /
Today's Energy_____
Intention_____
Today's Card_____

Dream
Keywords_____
_____.
Affirmations_____
_____.
Gratitude_____
_____.

Moon Phase:

My Practice:

•
•
•

Date: / /
Today's Energy_____
Intention_____
Today's Card_____

Dream
Keywords_____
_____.
Affirmations_____
_____.
Gratitude_____
_____.

Moon Phase:

My Practice:

•
•
•

Date: / /
Today's Energy_____
Intention_____
Today's Card_____

Dream
Keywords_____
_____.
Affirmations_____
_____.
Gratitude_____
_____.

Moon Phase:

My Practice:

.
.
.

Date: / /
Today's Energy_____
Intention_____
Today's Card_____

Dream
Keywords_____
_____.
Affirmations_____
_____.
Gratitude_____
_____.

Moon Phase:

My Practice:

.
.
.

Date: / /   Moon Phase:
Today's Energy_____
Intention_____
Today's Card_____

Dream
Keywords_____
_____.
                                     My Practice:
Affirmations_____   •
_____.   •
Gratitude_____   •
_____.

Date: / /   Moon Phase:
Today's Energy_____
Intention_____
Today's Card_____

Dream
Keywords_____
                                     My Practice:
_____.
Affirmations_____   •
_____.   •
Gratitude_____   •
_____.

Date: / /

Today's Energy_____

Intention_____

Today's Card_____

Dream
Keywords_____

_____.

Affirmations_____

_____.

Gratitude_____

_____.

Moon Phase:

My Practice:

•

•

•

Date: / /

Today's Energy_____

Intention_____

Today's Card_____

Dream
Keywords_____

_____.

Affirmations_____

_____.

Gratitude_____

_____.

Moon Phase:

My Practice:

•

•

•

Date: / /   Moon Phase:

Today's Energy_____

Intention_____

Today's Card_____

Dream

Keywords_____

_____.   My Practice:

Affirmations_____   •

_____.   •

Gratitude_____   •

_____.

Date: / /   Moon Phase:

Today's Energy_____

Intention_____

Today's Card_____

Dream

Keywords_____

_____.   My Practice:

Affirmations_____   •

_____.   •

Gratitude_____   •

_____.

58

Date: / /

Today's Energy_____

Intention_____

Today's Card_____

Dream

Keywords_____

_____.

Affirmations_____

_____.

Gratitude_____

_____.

Moon Phase:

My Practice:

•

•

•

Date: / /

Today's Energy_____

Intention_____

Today's Card_____

Dream

Keywords_____

_____.

Affirmations_____

_____.

Gratitude_____

_____.

Moon Phase:

My Practice:

•

•

•

Date: / /

Today's Energy_____

Intention_____

Today's Card_____

Dream

Keywords_____

_____.

Affirmations_____

_____.

Gratitude_____

_____.

Moon Phase:

My Practice:

•

•

•

Date: / /

Today's Energy_____

Intention_____

Today's Card_____

Dream

Keywords_____

_____.

Affirmations_____

_____.

Gratitude_____

_____.

Moon Phase:

My Practice:

•

•

•

Date: / /
Today's Energy_____
Intention_____
Today's Card_____

Dream
Keywords_____
_____.
Affirmations_____
_____.
Gratitude_____
_____.

Moon Phase:

My Practice:

•
•
•

Date: / /
Today's Energy_____
Intention_____
Today's Card_____

Dream
Keywords_____
_____.
Affirmations_____
_____.
Gratitude_____
_____.

Moon Phase:

My Practice:

•
•
•

Date: / /   Moon Phase:
Today's Energy_____
Intention_____
Today's Card_____

Dream
Keywords_____

_____.   My Practice:
Affirmations_____
                                          •
_____.   •
Gratitude_____   •

_____.

Date: / /   Moon Phase:
Today's Energy_____
Intention_____
Today's Card_____

Dream
Keywords_____

_____.   My Practice:
Affirmations_____
                                          •
_____.   •
Gratitude_____   •

_____.

Date: / /   Moon Phase:
Today's Energy_____
Intention_____
Today's Card_____

Dream
Keywords_____

_____
Affirmations_____   •   My Practice:

_____   •
Gratitude_____   •

_____

Date: / /   Moon Phase:
Today's Energy_____
Intention_____
Today's Card_____

Dream
Keywords_____

_____
Affirmations_____   •   My Practice:

_____   •
Gratitude_____   •

_____

63

Date: / /
Today's Energy_____
Intention_____
Today's Card_____

Dream
Keywords_____

_____.

Affirmations_____

_____.

Gratitude_____

_____.

Moon Phase:

My Practice:

·
·
·

Date: / /
Today's Energy_____
Intention_____
Today's Card_____

Dream
Keywords_____

_____.

Affirmations_____

_____.

Gratitude_____

_____.

Moon Phase:

My Practice:

·
·
·

Date: / /

Today's Energy_____

Intention_____

Today's Card_____

Dream
Keywords_____

_____

Affirmations_____

_____

Gratitude_____

_____

Moon Phase:

My Practice:

-
-
-

Date: / /

Today's Energy_____

Intention_____

Today's Card_____

Dream
Keywords_____

_____

Affirmations_____

_____

Gratitude_____

_____

Moon Phase:

My Practice:

-
-
-

Date: / /

Today's Energy_____

Intention_____

Today's Card_____

Dream

Keywords_____

_____

Affirmations_____

_____

Gratitude_____

_____

Moon Phase:

My Practice:

.

.

.

Date: / /

Today's Energy_____

Intention_____

Today's Card_____

Dream

Keywords_____

_____

Affirmations_____

_____

Gratitude_____

_____

Moon Phase:

My Practice:

.

.

.

Date: / /   Moon Phase:
Today's Energy_____
Intention_____
Today's Card_____

Dream
Keywords_____
                                     My Practice:
_____.
Affirmations_____   •
_____.   •
Gratitude_____   •
_____.

Date: / /   Moon Phase:
Today's Energy_____
Intention_____
Today's Card_____

Dream
Keywords_____
                                     My Practice:
_____.
Affirmations_____   •
_____.   •
Gratitude_____   •
_____.

67

Date: / /

Today's Energy_____

Intention_____

Today's Card_____

Dream
Keywords_____

_____.

Affirmations_____

_____.

Gratitude_____

_____.

Moon Phase:

My Practice:

·

·

·

Date: / /

Today's Energy_____

Intention_____

Today's Card_____

Dream
Keywords_____

_____.

Affirmations_____

_____.

Gratitude_____

_____.

Moon Phase:

My Practice:

·

·

·

Date: / /   Moon Phase:
Today's Energy_____
Intention_____
Today's Card_____

Dream
Keywords_____

_____.   My Practice:

Affirmations_____   •

_____.   •

Gratitude_____   •

_____.

Date: / /   Moon Phase:
Today's Energy_____
Intention_____
Today's Card_____

Dream
Keywords_____

_____.   My Practice:

Affirmations_____   •

_____.   •

Gratitude_____   •

_____.

Date: / /   Moon Phase:
Today's Energy_____
Intention_____
Today's Card_____

Dream
Keywords_____

_____.   My Practice:

Affirmations_____   •

_____.   •

Gratitude_____   •

_____.

Date: / /   Moon Phase:
Today's Energy_____
Intention_____
Today's Card_____

Dream
Keywords_____

_____.   My Practice:

Affirmations_____   •

_____.   •

Gratitude_____   •

_____.

Date: / /   Moon Phase:
Today's Energy_____
Intention_____
Today's Card_____

Dream
Keywords_____
_____.   My Practice:
Affirmations_____   •
_____.   •
Gratitude_____   •
_____.

Date: / /   Moon Phase:
Today's Energy_____
Intention_____
Today's Card_____

Dream
Keywords_____
_____.   My Practice:
Affirmations_____   •
_____.   •
Gratitude_____   •
_____.

71

Date: / /
Today's Energy_____
Intention_____
Today's Card_____

Dream
Keywords_____
_____.
Affirmations_____
_____.
Gratitude_____
_____.

Moon Phase:

My Practice:

.

.

.

Date: / /
Today's Energy_____
Intention_____
Today's Card_____

Dream
Keywords_____
_____.
Affirmations_____
_____.
Gratitude_____
_____.

Moon Phase:

My Practice:

.

.

.

72

Date: / /
Today's Energy_____
Intention_____
Today's Card_____

Dream
Keywords_____
_____.
Affirmations_____
_____.
Gratitude_____
_____.

Moon Phase:

My Practice:

•

•

•

Date: / /
Today's Energy_____
Intention_____
Today's Card_____

Dream
Keywords_____
_____.
Affirmations_____
_____.
Gratitude_____
_____.

Moon Phase:

My Practice:

•

•

•

73

Date: / /   Moon Phase:
Today's Energy_____
Intention_____
Today's Card_____

Dream
Keywords_____
_____.   My Practice:
Affirmations_____   .
_____.   .
Gratitude_____   .
_____.

Date: / /   Moon Phase:
Today's Energy_____
Intention_____
Today's Card_____

Dream
Keywords_____
_____.   My Practice:
Affirmations_____   .
_____.   .
Gratitude_____   .
_____.

74

Date: / /

Today's Energy_____

Intention_____

Today's Card _____

Dream
Keywords_____
_____ .

Affirmations_____
_____ .

Gratitude_____
_____ .

Moon Phase:

My Practice:

·
·
·

Date: / /

Today's Energy_____

Intention_____

Today's Card_____

Dream
Keywords_____
_____ .

Affirmations_____
_____ .

Gratitude_____
_____ .

Moon Phase:

My Practice:

·
·
·

Date: / /   Moon Phase:
Today's Energy_____
Intention_____
Today's Card_____

Dream
Keywords_____
_____.   My Practice:
Affirmations_____   .
_____.   .
Gratitude_____   .
_____.

Date: / /   Moon Phase:
Today's Energy_____
Intention_____
Today's Card_____

Dream
Keywords_____
_____.   My Practice:
Affirmations_____   .
_____.   .
Gratitude_____   .
_____.

Date: / /

Today's Energy_____

Intention_____

Today's Card_____

Dream

Keywords_____

_____.

Affirmations_____

_____.

Gratitude_____

_____.

Moon Phase:

My Practice:

•

•

•

Date: / /

Today's Energy_____

Intention_____

Today's Card_____

Dream

Keywords_____

_____.

Affirmations_____

_____.

Gratitude_____

_____.

Moon Phase:

My Practice:

•

•

•

Date: / /   Moon Phase:
Today's Energy_____
Intention_____
Today's Card_____

Dream
Keywords_____

_____.   My Practice:
Affirmations_____   •

_____.   •
Gratitude_____   •

_____.

Date: / /   Moon Phase:
Today's Energy_____
Intention_____
Today's Card_____

Dream
Keywords_____

_____.   My Practice:
Affirmations_____   •

_____.   •
Gratitude_____   •

_____.

78

Date: / /
Today's Energy_____
Intention_____
Today's Card_____

Dream
Keywords_____
_____.
Affirmations_____
_____.
Gratitude_____
_____.

Moon Phase:

My Practice:

- •
- •
- •

Date: / /
Today's Energy_____
Intention_____
Today's Card_____

Dream
Keywords_____
_____.
Affirmations_____
_____.
Gratitude_____
_____.

Moon Phase:

My Practice:

- •
- •
- •

Date: / /
Today's Energy_____
Intention_____
Today's Card_____

Dream
Keywords_____

_____.
Affirmations_____

_____.
Gratitude_____

_____.

Moon Phase:

My Practice:

·

·

·

Date: / /
Today's Energy_____
Intention_____
Today's Card_____

Dream
Keywords_____

_____.
Affirmations_____

_____.
Gratitude_____

_____.

Moon Phase:

My Practice:

·

·

·

Date: / /

Today's Energy_____

Intention_____

Today's Card_____

Dream
Keywords_____

_____.

Affirmations_____

_____.

Gratitude_____

_____.

Moon Phase:

My Practice:

•

•

•

Date: / /

Today's Energy_____

Intention_____

Today's Card_____

Dream
Keywords_____

_____.

Affirmations_____

_____.

Gratitude_____

_____.

Moon Phase:

My Practice:

•

•

•

Date: / /
Today's Energy_____
Intention_____
Today's Card_____

Dream
Keywords_____
_____.
Affirmations_____   •
_____.   •
Gratitude_____   •
_____.

Moon Phase:

My Practice:

Date: / /
Today's Energy_____
Intention_____
Today's Card_____

Dream
Keywords_____
_____.
Affirmations_____   •
_____.   •
Gratitude_____   •
_____.

Moon Phase:

My Practice:

82

Date: / /

Today's Energy_____

Intention_____

Today's Card_____

Dream
Keywords_____

_____.

Affirmations_____

_____.

Gratitude_____

_____.

Moon Phase:

My Practice:

.

.

.

Date: / /

Today's Energy_____

Intention_____

Today's Card_____

Dream
Keywords_____

_____.

Affirmations_____

_____.

Gratitude_____

_____.

Moon Phase:

My Practice:

.

.

.

Date: / /   Moon Phase:
Today's Energy_____
Intention_____
Today's Card_____

Dream
Keywords_____

_____.   My Practice:
Affirmations_____   .
_____.   .
Gratitude_____   .
_____.

Date: / /   Moon Phase:
Today's Energy_____
Intention_____
Today's Card_____

Dream
Keywords_____

_____.   My Practice:
Affirmations_____   .
_____.   .
Gratitude_____   .
_____.

84

Date: / /

Today's Energy_____

Intention_____

Today's Card_____

Dream

Keywords_____

_____

Affirmations_____

_____

Gratitude_____

_____

Moon Phase:

My Practice:

-
-
-

Date: / /

Today's Energy_____

Intention_____

Today's Card_____

Dream

Keywords_____

_____

Affirmations_____

_____

Gratitude_____

_____

Moon Phase:

My Practice:

-
-
-

Date: / /   Moon Phase:
Today's Energy_____
Intention_____
Today's Card_____

Dream
Keywords_____

_____.   My Practice:
Affirmations_____   .
_____.   .
Gratitude_____   .
_____.

Date: / /   Moon Phase:
Today's Energy_____
Intention_____
Today's Card_____

Dream
Keywords_____

_____.   My Practice:
Affirmations_____   .
_____.   .
Gratitude_____   .
_____.

86

Date: / /   Moon Phase:

Today's Energy_____

Intention_____

Today's Card_____

Dream

Keywords_____

_____.   My Practice:

Affirmations_____   •

_____.   •

Gratitude_____   •

_____.

Date: / /   Moon Phase:

Today's Energy_____

Intention_____

Today's Card_____

Dream

Keywords_____

_____.   My Practice:

Affirmations_____   •

_____.   •

Gratitude_____   •

_____.

Date: / /

Today's Energy_____

Intention_____

Today's Card_____

Dream

Keywords_____

_____.

Affirmations_____

_____.

Gratitude_____

_____.

Moon Phase:

My Practice:

·
·
·

Date: / /

Today's Energy_____

Intention_____

Today's Card_____

Dream

Keywords_____

_____.

Affirmations_____

_____.

Gratitude_____

_____.

Moon Phase:

My Practice:

·
·
·

Date: / /   Moon Phase:

Today's Energy_____

Intention_____

Today's Card_____

Dream

Keywords_____

_____.   My Practice:

Affirmations_____   .

_____.   .

Gratitude_____   .

_____.

Date: / /   Moon Phase:

Today's Energy_____

Intention_____

Today's Card_____

Dream

Keywords_____

_____.   My Practice:

Affirmations_____   .

_____.   .

Gratitude_____   .

_____.

Date: / /
Today's Energy_____
Intention_____
Today's Card_____

Dream
Keywords_____
_____.
Affirmations_____
_____.
Gratitude_____
_____.

Moon Phase:

My Practice:

•
•
•

Date: / /
Today's Energy_____
Intention_____
Today's Card_____

Dream
Keywords_____
_____.
Affirmations_____
_____.
Gratitude_____
_____.

Moon Phase:

My Practice:

•
•
•

Date: / /
Today's Energy_____
Intention_____
Today's Card_____

Dream
Keywords_____

_____

Affirmations_____

_____

Gratitude_____

_____

Moon Phase:

My Practice:
- •
- •
- •

Date: / /
Today's Energy_____
Intention_____
Today's Card_____

Dream
Keywords_____

_____

Affirmations_____

_____

Gratitude_____

_____

Moon Phase:

My Practice:
- •
- •
- •

Date: / /   Moon Phase:
Today's Energy_____
Intention_____
Today's Card_____

Dream
Keywords_____

_____.   My Practice:
Affirmations_____   •
_____.   •
Gratitude_____   •
_____.

Date: / /   Moon Phase:
Today's Energy_____
Intention_____
Today's Card_____

Dream
Keywords_____

_____.   My Practice:
Affirmations_____   •
_____.   •
Gratitude_____   •
_____.

Date: / /   Moon Phase:
Today's Energy_____
Intention_____
Today's Card_____

Dream
Keywords_____
_____.   My Practice:
Affirmations_____   •
_____.   •
Gratitude_____   •
_____.

Date: / /   Moon Phase:
Today's Energy_____
Intention_____
Today's Card_____

Dream
Keywords_____
_____.   My Practice:
Affirmations_____   •
_____.   •
Gratitude_____   •
_____.

93

Date: / /

Today's Energy_____

Intention_____

Today's Card_____

Dream
Keywords_____

_____.

Affirmations_____

_____.

Gratitude_____

_____.

Moon Phase:

My Practice:

-
-
-

Date: / /

Today's Energy_____

Intention_____

Today's Card_____

Dream
Keywords_____

_____.

Affirmations_____

_____.

Gratitude_____

_____.

Moon Phase:

My Practice:

-
-
-

Date: / /

Today's Energy_____

Intention_____

Today's Card_____

Dream
Keywords_____

_____.

Affirmations_____

_____.

Gratitude_____

_____.

Moon Phase:

My Practice:

•

•

•

Date: / /

Today's Energy_____

Intention_____

Today's Card_____

Dream
Keywords_____

_____.

Affirmations_____

_____.

Gratitude_____

_____.

Moon Phase:

My Practice:

•

•

•

Date: / /

Today's Energy_____

Intention_____

Today's Card _____

Dream

Keywords_____

_____.

Affirmations_____

_____.

Gratitude_____

_____.

Moon Phase:

My Practice:

.

.

.

Reflections

_____
_____
_____
_____
_____
_____
_____
_____
_____
_____
_____
_____.

Full Moons

New Moons

Imbolc

Ostara

Beltane

Litha

Lughnasadh

Mabon

Samhain

Yule

.

Divination Notes

Reading Notes

Made in the USA
Las Vegas, NV
25 June 2023